MARILYN™
IN HER OWN WORDS

MARILYN ™
IN HER OWN WORDS

Compiled by Neil Grant

CRESCENT

EDITOR: JANICE ANDERSON, ART EDITOR: ROBIN WHITECROSS
PICTURE RESEARCH: EMILY HEDGES
PRODUCTION: ALYSSUM ROSS

THIS 1991 EDITION PUBLISHED BY CRESCENT BOOKS,
DISTRIBUTED BY OUTLET BOOK COMPANY INC.,
A RANDOM HOUSE COMPANY,
225 PARK AVENUE SOUTH, NEW YORK, NEW YORK 10003

"MARILYN MONROE" IS A TRADEMARK OF THE ESTATE OF MARILYN MONROE

COMPILATION AND DESIGN © 1991 REED INTERNATIONAL BOOKS LTD

ISBN 0 517 06103 1

8 7 6 5 4 3 2 1

PRINTED AND BOUND IN HONG KONG

CONTENTS

AS YOUNG AS YOU FEEL

*"No-one ever told me I was pretty
when I was a little girl. All little girls should be told
they are pretty, even if they aren't"*

Although Marilyn Monroe became the most fabulous sex symbol of the Western World, she was never a remote, Garbo-like goddess, wearing her sexuality like a suit of armor, nor a slinky, diamond-eyed siren from a marble palazzo, equally unattainable to John Doe and his pals. She was gorgeous, she was a superstar, but she was also – it was part of her charm – like the girl from next door.

Norma Jean's background was murky in more ways than one. She never knew who her father was, and her mother, like most of her family, suffered bouts of mental disturbance serious enough for her to be institutionalized. Even when she was well she had to work full-time, and little Norma Jean was boarded out with foster-parents. They treated her well and, apart from at least one sharp experience with a strap, kindly. Norma Jean was not a poor, hungry or neglected child, but at six years old life is still far from perfect when you are confused about who you should call "Mommy".

After the foster parents came the orphanage. That was a real shock. The year was 1935, Norma Jean was nine, and her mother had been admitted to the asylum for a long spell. It was then that the little girl, hating the orphanage (by all accounts a good one) and unable to understand what she was doing there when she had a mother, began to retreat into the fantasy which years later was to become reality. Probably most little girls in the 1930s, especially unhappy little girls, dreamed of becoming a film star, and for Norma Jean, who lived in Los Angeles and had often goggled at the stars from the sidewalk outside Grauman's Chinese Theater, the dream was not so fantastic.

At high school, no-one took much notice of her and no hidden talents, dramatic or others, were revealed, but Norma Jean discovered that she could attract instant attention very easily – simply by wearing a sweater. She was soon to be seen at the soda fountain or on the beach, surrounded by young male admirers. The woman she lived

with for a time at the age of fifteen, Ana Lower, a devout Christian to whom Norma Jean was sufficiently committed to take up churchgoing, became more than a little alarmed. So did her niece, a friend of Norma's mother and the girl's legal guardian. One way to prevent likely trouble ahead was marriage. A pleasant young fellow was found, he fell for the lively and strikingly attractive sixteen-year-old according to plan, and in 1942, the first year of America's involvement in the World War, they were married.

It might perhaps have worked. Jim Dougherty did not like the way other men looked at his young wife and he did not approve of her ambition to get into movies,

but what doomed the relationship was Jim's posting overseas. Norma Jean, working in an aircraft factory (she looked good in overalls too), was asked to pose for pin-ups in Yank magazine: she was on her way. A model agency took her on, she turned (a little reluctantly) into a blonde, she worked hard and conscientiously (acquiring her notorious choosiness over what shots of her should be printed), and she filed for divorce. Ben Lyon, then a Hollywood agent, signed her up, and got her a screen test with Twentieth Century-Fox. The test looked good (though so did the tests of dozens of other young hopefuls), and the studio put her under contract. "Norma Jean Mortensen" (the name on her birth certificate, which derived from one of her mother's lovers – almost certainly not Norma Jean's father) did not strike any sparks, so after much discussion the twenty-year-old apprentice starlet became, as all the world would know her, Marilyn Monroe.

As Marilyn Monroe turned fantasy into reality, so she tended to turn reality into fantasy. In her own account, her childhood was much grimmer than her biographers have found it to be. She saw herself as the heroine of a rags-to-riches fairytale, and adjusted the facts accordingly. Which was tough on a lot of people who had been decent to her.

"You see, I was brought up differently from the average American child, because the average child is brought up expecting to be happy."

"My marriage [to Jim Dougherty] brought me neither happiness nor pain. My husband and I hardly spoke to each other. This wasn't because we were angry. We had nothing to say."

*"Some of my foster families used to send me
to the movies to get me out of the house, and I'd sit all day
and way into the night...I loved anything that moved up there
and I didn't miss anything that happened-
and there was no popcorn either!"*

*"I dreamed of myself walking proudly
in beautiful clothes and being admired by everyone and
overhearing words of praise."*

"I'm going to be a great movie star some day" (1946)

*"I've tried to pick up all the camera experience I can around
the photographers who've used me."*

*"The truth was that with all my lipstick and mascara
and precocious curves I was as unresponsive as a fossil...
I used to lie awake at night wondering why
the boys came after me."*

THERE'S NO BUSINESS LIKE SHOW BUSINESS

"Only the public can make a star.
It's the studios who try to make a system out of it"

For two years Marilyn went through the usual routine of the aspiring Hollywood starlet – endless photo sessions and publicity appearances. She went to the right kind of restaurant with the right kind of escort and was sent to classes in singing, dancing and acting – which she took very seriously. She even had a couple of bit parts in films, too small for the sharpest talent-spotter to notice; but when her contract was up, the studio did not renew it.

Then came the lean years, when she lived off modelling jobs and made love, selectively, to men who might be useful. Columbia took her up for a time and sent her to acting classes with Natasha Lytess, who became a close friend and counselor for many years. She had a small but glamorous role in *Ladies of the Chorus* and an affair with Columbia's music director, who taught her how to sing. In 1949 she posed nude for a calendar entitled "Golden Dreams" and, soon afterwards, landed a tiny part in a Marx Bros movie called *Love Happy*, the swaying of her hips as she walked across the room having clinched it for Groucho Marx. Her performance attracted top agent Johnny Hyde who, spurred by love as well as professional belief, worked his heart out for her. He had less than two years to live, but he got her back on Fox's books, had her teeth straightened and her nose trimmed a little, and smoothed down her brash cheesecake image. Best of all, he got her parts in two outstanding films, John Huston's *The Asphalt Jungle* and Joseph Mankiewicz's *All About Eve*, in which she had a small part as a "dumb blonde" actress, a type she often played – too often? – to such perfection that people sometimes supposed, quite wrongly, that she was a "dumb blonde" herself.

All About Eve, with six Oscars, was a great

15

"I don't understand why people aren't a little more generous with each other"

success, but her part was a small one and it did not lead to instant stardom. She played in a number of much less distinguished pictures, and she continued to model for girlie shots, while attending courses on art at the University of Southern California.

What made the movie moguls sit up and take notice at last was the volume of her fan mail and the nationwide popular interest that sprang, partly at least, from her pin-up work. The Fox studio, famous for its gorgeous blondes (Betty Grable, June Haver, Lana Turner, now past their best), gave her more substantial parts in *As Young as You Feel*, for which she gained good reviews from several serious serious critics, *Love Nest* and *Let's Make It Legal*.

All were fairly feeble comedies, but Marilyn gained useful experience and greater fame. When someone recognized her as the girl in the "Golden Dreams" calendar she was nearly sacked, but in the end notoriety is as good as more conventional

publicity. Marilyn dealt with the problem with dewy-eyed candor and the less than candid confession, when asked why she had done it, that her motive had been "hunger". Did she have anything on at the time? – "The radio".

Though she'd had nothing but small parts, by 1952 Marilyn was a rising star. The studio recognized it, and so did the gossip columnists: Marilyn was news. The question remained, was she an actress, or only a sex object? She insisted she was a serious performer, while the studio showed its doubts by continuing to cast her in small frothy roles. One exception was *Don't Bother to Knock*, in which she played a babysitter with homicidal urges, but the film was not a great success and she returned to lightweight glamour-girls. In *Niagara*, a steamy tale of sex and murder, Marilyn got her first juicy part, and made the most of it. Not every critic was convinced, but the public was and as Marilyn said, it's the public that makes a star.

*"My illusions didn't have anything to do
with being a fine actress. I knew how third-rate I was.
I could actually feel my lack of talent, as if it were cheap clothes
I was wearing inside. But, my God, how I wanted to learn,
to change, to improve! I didn't want anything else.
Not men, not money, not love, but the ability to act"* (1949)

"I had to wiggle across a room.
I practiced jiggling my backside for a week.
Groucho loved it."

"I learned to walk as a baby
and I haven't had a lesson since."

"I think if other girls know how
bad I was when I started they'll be encouraged.
I finally made up my mind I wanted
to be an actress and I was not going to let my
lack of confidence ruin my chances."

"He [Johnny Hyde] not only knew me,
he knew Norma Jean too.
He knew all the pain and all the desperate things in me.
When he put his arms around me
and said he loved me, I knew it was true.
Nobody had ever loved me like that."

Best wishes
Marilyn Mon

*"My impulses [as a little girl]
to appear naked had no shame or sense
of sin in them. I think I wanted
people to see me naked because I was
ashamed of the clothes I wore.
Naked, I was like other girls and not
someone in an orphan's uniform."*

*"People have curious attitudes
about nudity, just as they have about
sex. Nudity and sex are the most
commonplace things in the world.
Yet people often act as if they were
things that existed only on Mars."*

*"My sin has been no more
than I have written —
posing for the nude picture because
I needed fifty dollars desperately
to get my automobile out of hock."*

GENTLEMEN PREFER BLONDES

*"I am not interested in money.
I just want to be wonderful"*

Marilyn Monroe made about 30 films, but only a handful of them are good films in which she had a starring part. In *Gentlemen Prefer Blondes* she starred with Jane Russell as two nightclub entertainers on the make. It is an amusing musical comedy, with some wit, several good song-and-dance numbers and outstandingly glamorous costumes. Though not received with much enthusiasm by the critics, it has worn well – and it made plenty of money. Perhaps surprisingly, as Jane Russell was being paid much more and Marilyn had trouble getting a suitable dressing room, the two stars got along very well on and off set, but the first signs of future trouble (including a neurotic compulsion to be late on set) appeared in Marilyn's fights with the director, Howard Hawks.

Jane and Marilyn appeared together to have their handprints and footprints set in concrete outside Grauman's Chinese Theater; Marilyn was also voted by Photoplay as the "most promising newcomer" of 1953 – after seven years in the business!

How To Marry A Millionaire was in the same vein. Again, trouble might have been expected between Marilyn (given top billing) and Betty Grable, her predecessor as Hollywood's most valuable blonde, but Grable mothered her. The film, in which Marilyn appeared in glasses – and in a famous gold lamé dress – was a big success. ·

It was followed by *River of No Return*, filmed in the Canadian Rockies (with Robert Mitchum), which proved an exhausting and unhappy experience. Marilyn returned to civilization in a bitter mood. She refused to make *The Girl in Pink Tights* (which sounds like a wise decision), in which she would have co-starred with

*"The only thing was I couldn't get a dressing room.
I said finally...'Look, after all I **am** the blonde
and it **is Gentlemen Prefer Blondes'"**

Frank Sinatra (a future lover), and was suspended by the studio.

Because she was now one of the biggest attractions in Hollywood, if not **the** biggest, it was not long before she was back before the cameras. *There's No Business Like Show Business* was a crudish vehicle for the songs of Irving Berlin, and Marilyn was cast with top singers (like Ethel Merman, famous for her "big" voice just as Marilyn was for her "little" one) and dancers (Dan Dailey, Mitzi Gaynor and Donald O'Connor, perhaps the best Hollywood dancer after Astaire). Irving Berlin approved of the way Marilyn sung his songs, but her brash and sexy performance did not do her much good at a time when she was more than ever set on becoming a serious actress.

With *The Seven Year Itch* she was back on the right track. A witty comedy by George Axelrod, directed by Billy Wilder, it was ideal for her, and most reviewers admitted that Monroe was a really talented actress in comedy. "She makes sex funny", one said. That is an even harder thing than – another gift of Marilyn's – making sex fun.

She confirmed her reputation with the bitter-sweet comedy, *Bus Stop* , with screenplay again by Axelrod and directed by Joshua Logan, a distinguished man of the theatre. The smalltime cafe singer who dreams of the big time but settles for cosy housewifery was a perfect part for her (though she antagonized her leading man, Don Murray). Some of the sharpest critics say that *Bus Stop* was her best picture.

"It is a woman's spirit and mood a man
has to stimulate in order to make sex interesting.
The real lover is the man who can thrill you
by touching your head or smiling into your eyes
or by just staring into space."

"I feel as though it's all happening to
someone right next to me.
I'm close, I can feel it, I can hear it,
but it isn't really me."

"There was my name, up in lights.
I said, 'God, somebody's made
a mistake.' But there it was, in lights.
And I sat there and said,
'Remember you're not a star.'
Yet there it was up in lights."

"That's the trouble –
a sex symbol becomes a thing.
I just hate being a thing.
But if I'm going to be a symbol
of something, I'd rather
have it sex than some other things
we've got symbols of."

"Success came to me in a rush.
It surprised my employers much more than it did me."

"Fame is not really for a daily diet.
That's not what fulfills you. It warms you a bit, but
the warming is temporary. It's like caviare,
but not when you have it every meal."

"It stirs up envy, fame does.
People you run into feel that, well, who is she?
Who does she think she is, Marilyn Monroe?
They feel fame gives them some kind of privilege to
walk up to you and say anything
to you – and it won't hurt your feelings – like it's
happening to your clothing."

"I think that sexuality is only attractive
when its natural and spontaneous.
We are born sexual creatures, thank God,
but it's a pity so many people
despise and crush this natural gift."

"Sex is part of nature.
I go along with nature."

"[When making a movie]
there's no audience watching you.
There's nobody to act for
except yourself. It's like the games
you play when you are a
child and pretend to be someone
else. Usually, it's almost
the same sort of story you made
up as a child."

"I feel stronger if the people around
me on the set love me, care
for me, and hold good thoughts for
me. It creates an aura of love,
and I believe I can give a better
performance."

"Sometimes in the evening,
I wish there was someone to take
me out who doesn't expect
anything from me.
You know what I mean?"

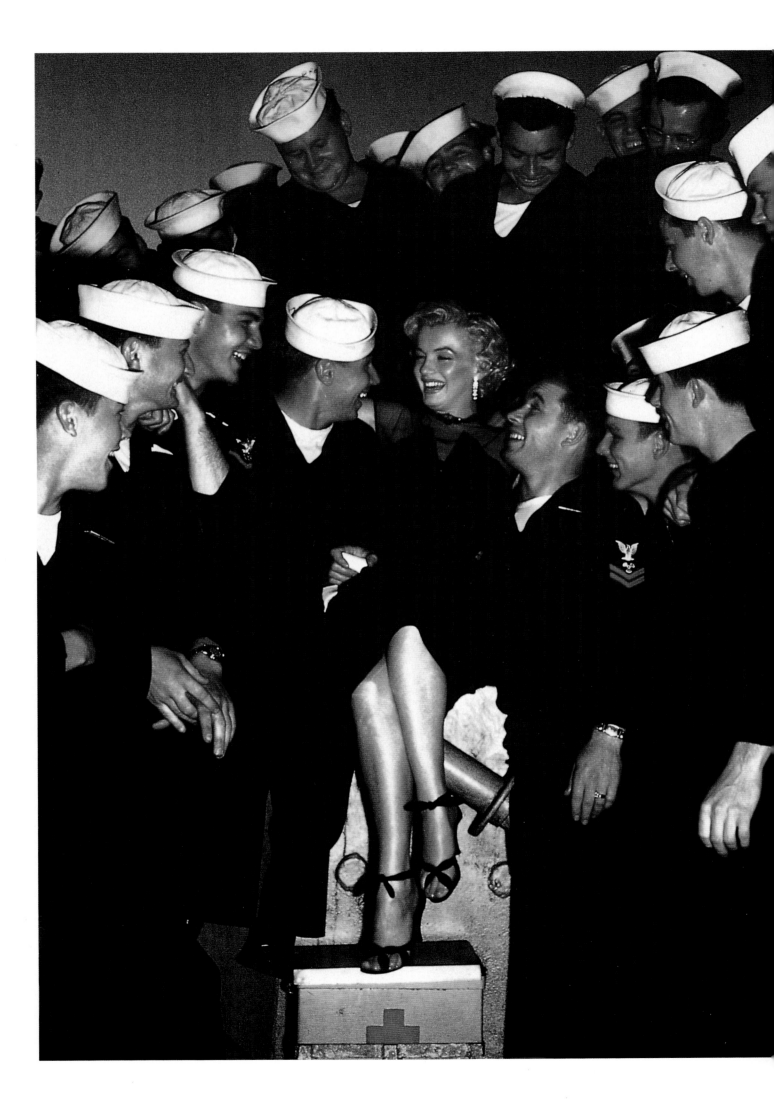

THE SEVEN YEAR ITCH

"A career is wonderful,

but you can't curl up with a career on a cold night"

Marilyn was reticent, even deceitful, about some aspects of life – much of her love life remains a mystery – but in a sense a star, at least a star as big as she was, has no private life. Just as his or her effectiveness as a performer depends on an indivisible combination of acting talent and personality, so the star's "private" life is also part of the performance.

Discounting her teenage alliance with Jim Dougherty, Marilyn Monroe, the greatest American popular heroine of her time, made two marriages, neatly representing Mind and Body – the greatest contemporary player of America's national game and (maybe) its greatest playwright. She could have married anybody – even, perhaps, Prince Rainier of Monaco, when

he was combing the film studios for a beautiful consort.

While making *River of No Return* Marilyn injured her leg. Dissatisfied with her treatment and generally unhappy, she put in a call to her friend, the famous ex-baseball player Joe DiMaggio. He arrived post haste with a doctor. Marilyn was touched and agreed to marry him when he asked her.

They had been going out for some time, to the joy of gossip columnists and publicity agents, and their marriage was greeted with popular celebration: America's greatest athlete weds America's greatest film star. Symbolically it was fine; in reality it was disastrous. DiMaggio was to prove a loyal and devoted friend to the end, but he was a conservative, conventional, middle-aged,

"I always keep my undies in the icebox"

American male. He would have liked her to stay home and cook pasta: he had no use for Hollywood and even less for the world of glamour. He hated the idea of thousands of soldiers leering at his wife when she did a brief tour in Korea. He was disgusted by the scene in *The Seven Year Itch* when, watched by a New York crowd, a giggling Marilyn allowed the breeze from the subway to blow her skirt up. The fairytale marriage lasted less than a year.

Perhaps Joe helped to put her off her sexy-blonde image, for she became even more serious about her career. With the aid and support of Milton Greene, a fashion photographer and, for two or three years, a close friend, she formed Marilyn Monroe Productions. To the even greater astonishment of Hollywood, she moved to New York to take lessons from Lee Strasberg, the head of the Actors Studio.

It was an act as courageous as it was surprising. Strasberg took her seriously, believed she had real talent, and his wife Paula became a powerful influence, replacing the loyal Natasha Lytess as Marilyn's ever-present (except when banned from the film set by irate directors) drama coach.

In the summer he accompanied her to England, where Marilyn Monroe Productions were to make *The Prince and the Showgirl* with Marilyn and Laurence Olivier – another unlikely partnership. The film is flimsy but amusing, but the trip was not a success. Marilyn was in poor health – she had long ago become dependent on various drugs – and for once she missed her step publicity-wise, slightly alienating the British press. Nor did she get along with the great English classical actor/director either. Olivier later admitted with evident restraint that she was "difficult to work with"

*"I guess I never felt I had an effect on people
until I was in Korea."*

*"I don't know why you boys [U.S. Marines bound
for Korea] are always getting so excited about sweater girls.
Take away their sweaters and what have you got?"*

"Men feel as if they want to spend all night with me."

*"I knew I belonged
to the public and to the world,
not because I was talented
or even beautiful, but because
I had never belonged to
anything or anyone else"*

"He [DiMaggio] was shy and reserved
but, at the same time, rather warm and friendly.
I noticed that he wasn't eating the food in front of him,
that he was looking at me."

"I'm an old-fashioned girl who believes a husband and wife
should share the same bedroom and bed."

"He [DiMaggio] didn't talk to me. He was cold.
He was indifferent to me as a human being and an artist.
He didn't want me to have friends of my own.
He didn't want me to do my work. He watched television
instead of talking to me."

"I've never followed baseball."

"I realized that just as I had once fought to get
into the movies and become an actress,
I would now have to fight to become myself and
be able to use my talents."

"All I want is to play something different.
The Strasbergs say I can."

"In many respects I'd like to become more mature:
But that takes time, and you've got to work at it steadily...
I want to be the best actress I can be."

"It's easier to look sexy
when you are thinking of one man in particular."

"Arthur [Miller] is a serious man,
but he has a wonderful sense of humor.
We laugh and joke a lot."

"This is the first time I think I've really been in love."

"It was like running into a tree! You know, like a cool drink when you've got a fever. You see my toe? Well, he [Miller] sat and held my toe and we just looked into each other's eyes almost all evening."

"He [Miller] wouldn't have married me if I had been nothing but a dumb blonde."

"Movies are my business but Arthur is my life."

"He [Laurence Olivier] gave
me the dirtiest looks, even when he
was smiling."

"I hope you will all forgive me.
It wasn't my fault.
I've been very, very sick all
through the picture.
Please – please
don't hold it against me."

FAREWELL SPEECH TO THE CAST OF *THE PRINCE AND THE SHOWGIRL*

SOMETHING'S GOT TO GIVE

"I don't want to play sex roles anymore.
I'm tired of being known as the girl with the shape"

For a year or two the Miller-Monroe marriage not only worked, it purred. Everyone noticed how much they were in love. Unfortunately, though, the expected outcome – babies – did not appear. Marilyn got pregnant twice but both had to be terminated. A minor gynecological operation failed to cure the problem, and the failed pregnancies drove her deep into depression.

Work might have helped but did not. Miller helped to persuade her to make *Some Like It Hot* in 1958, with Tony Curtis and Jack Lemon, directed by Billy Wilder. It is one of the funniest films ever made, but without Marilyn's wonderful portrayal of innocent sexuality, it might have been no more than a drag queen's giggle. During the making of the film, though, Marilyn drove Billy Wilder near to breakdown and antagonized almost everyone else. Tony Curtis made his notorious remark that kissing Marilyn was "like kissing Hitler".

More trouble dogged the making of *Let's Make Love* with Yves Montand, though it was less bad, perhaps because Marilyn fell for Montand's Gallic charm (which, together with Marilyn's rendering of "My Heart Belongs To Daddy" dressed in a heavy wool sweater and tights, is the main attraction of this feeble romantic comedy).

The Montand affair confirmed that Marilyn's marriage was in trouble, and everything fell apart during the making of *The Misfits*. Ironically, the screenplay was written by Miller specially for Marilyn, but he adapted it from his short story about three cowboys, played in the film by Clark Gable, Montgomery Clift and Eli Wallach, in which the Monroe part is insignificant. In the hands of John Huston the film, too, is really about the three cowboys.

It is surprising that Marilyn was as good

"I don't mind making jokes, but I don't want to look like one"

as she was, because she was near to collapse. She was now so dependent on drugs that often she could barely speak her lines, let alone memorize them (sometimes her lines were posted where she could see them but the camera couldn't). The only bright spot was that one of her childhood idols, Clark Gable, lived up to her image of him. Sadly, he died a few weeks after filming ended.

Meanwhile, Marilyn went to Mexico for a divorce. Joe DiMaggio, "Mr Dependable", came into the picture again, flying to New York to rescue her from a mental clinic into which her doctor had inveigled her, and taking her down to Florida to watch the Yankees in a spring training session.

Despite unwelcome attention from the world press ("Golden Goddess Cracks Up!"), she seemed to make a good recovery. She bought a house in Hollywood, had an affair with Frank Sinatra, and flew to to New York City to sing "Happy Birthday to You" for President John Kennedy at his birthday celebrations.

Unfortunately, this celebration took place while Marilyn was supposed to be filming *Something's Got To Give*. All the old problems recurred. Marilyn was by now incapable of enough self-discipline to make a film. The studio fired her, and the film was scrapped. Almost all that remains of it is a nude bathing scene, which reveals that, physically, Marilyn was still in very good shape.

During the night of 4/5 August 1962, Marilyn died of an overdose. It was not the first time she had put her life in danger, but this time help was not at hand. Whether she killed herself deliberately or accidentally is a meaningless question.

"He [Tony Curtis] only said that about 'kissing Hitler' because
I wore prettier dresses than he did."

"I am invariably late for appointments —
sometimes as much as two hours. I've tried to change my ways
but the things that make me late are too strong,
and too pleasing."

"Next to my husband and along with Marlon Brando,
Yves Montand is the most attractive man I've ever met."

"Men who think that a woman's past love
affairs lessen her love for them are usually stupid and weak.
A woman can bring a new love to each man she loves,
providing there are not too many."

*"He [John Huston] treats me
like an idiot –
'Honey this' – and 'Honey that'."*

*"He [Clark Gable] never got angry
with me once for blowing a line
or being late or anything.
He was a gentleman – the best."*

*"He [Montgomery Clift] is the
only person I know who's in worse
shape than I am."*

56

*"He [Miller] is a wonderful writer,
a brilliant man. But I think he
is a better writer than a husband."*

*"He [Miller] could have written me
anything. If that's what he thinks
of me, well,then I'm not for him and
he's not for me."*

*"It's better to be unhappy alone than
unhappy with someone."*

"Everybody [in crowds] is always tugging at you.
They'd all like a sort of chunk out of you.
I don't think they realize it, but it's like 'rrrr do this,
rrrr do that...' but you do want to stay intact —
intact and on two feet."

"What am I afraid of? Why am I so afraid?
Do I think I can't act? I know I can act but I am afraid.
I am afraid and I should not be and I must not be."

<small>FROM A PRIVATE NOTEBOOK (1959)</small>

"We did some test scenes of me in a pool,
sort of nude. I hope they give me some good nude lines
to go with it."

"[Acting is] a real struggle.
I'm one of the world's most self-conscious people.
I really have to struggle."

"I'm looking forward to eventually becoming a marvelous —
excuse the word marvelous — character actress."

"The truth is I've never fooled anyone.
I've sometimes let men fool themselves."

"I love to do the things the censors won't pass.
After all, what are we all here for? Just to stand around
and let it pass us by?"

"If I'd observed all the rules, I'd never have got anywhere."

"She [a character in a play] was a girl
who knew how to be gay even when she was sad.
And that's important - you know?"

PICTURE CREDITS

PAGE 1: Marilyn Monroe does some high-level publicity work for *As Young As You Feel* (Twentieth Century-Fox, 1951). **THE KOBAL COLLECTION**

PAGE 2: An image perfected: Marilyn as cinema's most famous blonde, *c.* 1953. **PICTORIAL PRESS**

PAGE 6: An early modelling shot, *c.* 1947. **PICTORIAL PRESS**

PAGE 7: Norma Jean Mortensen as a baby. **REX FEATURES**

PAGE 8: 16-years-old Norma Jean and husband Jim Dougherty on their wedding day, June 1942. **PICTORIAL PRESS**

PAGE 9: An early modelling pose, mid-1940s. **TOPHAM PICTURE LIBRARY**

PAGE 10: Scene from Marilyn's first movie, *Dangerous Years* (Twentieth Century-Fox, 1947). **THE KOBAL COLLECTION**

PAGE 11: Publicity pose, *c.* 1948. **REX FEATURES**

PAGE 12: Finding the perfect angle for a photograph by Joseph Jasgur, *c.* 1949. **REX FEATURES**

PAGE 13: Marilyn, *c.* 1950. **PICTORIAL PRESS**

PAGE 14: There is an innocent look in Marilyn's eyes, in this publicity shot from 1950. **THE RONALD GRANT ARCHIVE**

PAGE 15: Rising young movie starlet posing for photographer André de Dienes on Jones Beach, New York, in 1950. **REX FEATURES**

PAGE 16: Marilyn posing in a swimsuit, *c.* 1950. **PICTORIAL PRESS**

PAGE 17: A fresh, outdoors look for Marilyn in this photograph by Bruno Bernard *c.* 1950. **PICTORIAL PRESS**

PAGE 18: Philippe Halsman took this photograph of the Monroe walk in 1952; it later became a famous poster. **MAGNUM PHOTOS**

PAGE 19: A sophisticated Marilyn is on view in this publicity picture of the early 1950s. **REX FEATURES**

PAGES 20–21 1950 glamour pose: Marilyn in the style of Lana Turner. **THE KOBAL COLLECTION**

PAGE 22: In this picture, photographed by Gene Kornman in 1953, the gold lamé dress Marilyn wears was to become almost as famous as its wearer. **THE KOBAL COLLECTION**

PAGE 23: The high-octane star of *Gentlemen Prefer Blondes* (Twentieth Century-Fox, 1953). **THE RONALD GRANT ARCHIVE**

PAGE 24: Marilyn and Jane Russell shape up for *Gentlemen Prefer Blondes*. **THE KOBAL COLLECTION**

PAGE 25: Publicity shot for *How to Marry A Millionaire* (Twentieth Century-Fox, 1953). **THE KOBAL COLLECTION**

PAGES 26–7: Marilyn seductive in black lace. **THE KOBAL COLLECTION**

PAGE 29: Marilyn gives Irving Berlin everything she's got in *There's No Business Like Show Business* (Twentieth Century-Fox, 1954). **REX FEATURES**

PAGE 30: Monroe photographed by Milton Greene in Los Angeles, 1955. **CAMERA PRESS**

PAGE 31: Shot from *The Seven Year Itch* (Twentieth Century-Fox,1955). **PICTORIAL PRESS**

PAGES 32-3: A series of pictures taken by Philippe Halsman for Life magazine in 1952. **MAGNUM PHOTOS**

PAGE 34: Marilyn surrounded by enthusiastic US servicemen. **LONDON FEATURES INTERNATIONAL**

PAGE 35: The Girl falls off her neighbour's piano stool: scene from *The Seven Year Itch*. **THE KOBAL COLLECTION**

PAGE 36: Entertaining the troops in Korea, 1954. **THE RONALD GRANT ARCHIVE.**

PAGE 37: A publicity appearance for *The Seven Year Itch*, Yankee Stadium, New York, 1954, photographed by Bob Henriques. **MAGNUM PHOTOS**

PAGES 38-9: Marilyn takes the minds of US forces in Korea off the war, 1954. **TOPHAM PICTURE LIBRARY**

PAGE 40: Mr and Mrs Joe DiMaggio after their marriage in New York, January 1954. **LAWRENCE SCHILLER (CAMERA PRESS)**

PAGE 41: The most famous Monroe pin-up of them all: photograph by Sam Shaw of The Girl standing on a subway grating in *The Seven Year Itch*, New York 1954. Tom Ewell looks on. **LAWRENCE SCHILLER (CAMERA PRESS)**

PAGE 42: Marilyn photographed by Bob Henriques during filming of *The Seven Year Itch*. **MAGNUM PHOTOS**

PAGE 43: Marilyn photographed by Sam Shaw in New York, 1954. **LAWRENCE SCHILLER (CAMERA PRESS)**

PAGE 44: Marilyn and Arthur Miller pause for a photograph by Sam Shaw, New York, 1956. **LAWRENCE SCHILLER (CAMERA PRESS)**

PAGE 45: Marilyn's friend and business partner, Milton Greene, took this picture in New York in 1954. **LAWRENCE SCHILLER (CAMERA PRESS)**

PAGES 46-7: Marilyn and Arthur Miller enjoying life at their summer retreat at Amagansett. Photograph by Sam Shaw. **PICTORIAL PRESS**

PAGE 47: Cycling in the English countryside with Arthur Miller, 1956. **THE HULTON PICTURE COMPANY**

PAGE 48: Monroe with Sir Laurence Olivier, about to make *The Prince and the Showgirl* (Warner Brothers, 1957). **THE KOBAL COLLECTION**

PAGE 49: Eve Arnold photograped Monroe and Olivier during the press conference in the Waldorf Astoria Ballroom, New York, to announce the making of *The Prince and the Showgirl* in England. **MAGNUM PHOTOS**

PAGE 50. Marilyn as Sugar Kane in *Some Like It Hot* (United Artists, 1959). **LONDON FEATURES INTERNATIONAL**

PAGE 51: Photograph by Milton Greene, New York, 1956. **CAMERA PRESS**

PAGE 52: Monroe and Tony Curtis manage bright smiles for each other off the set of *Some Like It Hot*. **THE RONALD GRANT ARCHIVE**

PAGE 53: Running for the boat, *Some Like It Hot*. **REX FEATURES**

PAGE 54: Marilyn with Yves Montand in *Let's Make Love* (Twentieth Century-Fox, 1960). Photograph by Lawrence Schiller. **CAMERA PRESS**

PAGE 55: Marilyn boosting the Aran sweater industry while singing Cole Porter's "My Heart Belongs to Daddy" in *Let's Make Love*. **THE HULTON PICTURE COMPANY**

PAGE 56: Publicity picture for *The Misfits* (United Artists, 1961) including, clockwise from Marilyn, Montgomery Clift, film's producer Frank Taylor, Eli Wallach, Arthur Miller, John Huston, Clark Gable. **THE KOBAL COLLECTION**

PAGES 56-7: Marilyn as Roslyn Tabor in *The Misfits*: photograph by Eve Arnold. **MAGNUM PHOTOS**

PAGES 58-9: Off-set shot by Inge Morath during shooting of *The Misfits*. **MAGNUM PHOTOS**

PAGE 59: Marilyn and Arthur Miller in conference between takes for *The Misfits*: photograph by Eve Arnold. **MAGNUM PHOTOS**

PAGE 60: Marilyn mobbed by the press, New York, November 1960. **POPPERFOTO**

PAGE 61: Still from the test scenes for *Something's Got to Give*, 1962. **LAWRENCE SCHILLER (CAMERA PRESS)**

PAGE 62: Bert Stern took this dramatic picture of Marilyn Monroe during the last weeks of her life, 1962. **LAWRENCE SCHILLER (CAMERA PRESS)**

PAGE 63: Portrait by Douglas Kirkland, 1962 **THE RONALD GRANT ARCHIVE**

ALTHOUGH EVERY EFFORT HAS BEEN MADE TO TRACE THE COPYRIGHT HOLDER, WE APOLOGISE IN ADVANCE FOR ANY UNINTENTIONAL OMISSIONS AND WOULD BE PLEASED TO INSERT THE APPROPRIATED ACKNOWLEDGEMENTS IN ANY SUBSEQUENT EDITION OF THIS PUBLICATION.